Robin Re

The British Robin
My Little Nature Books - Book 1
2nd Edition

Author's Introduction to the Series

In this new series of "Little Nature Books" I hope to pass on something of the enjoyment I have experienced in recent years. I've wandered around woodland, along seashores and by lakes and ponds. Training myself to keep my eyes open, at first for birds and then more with my camera at the ready, has led to new pleasures.

At first it was only an occasional walk for relaxation, but it soon became a serious hobby. I've enjoyed learning about the birds and other wildlife in my photographs, and have been encouraged by friends to share what I have learned.

Further books are planned, including:

Goldfinches and other Finches

Butterflies and Moths

Blackbirds and other Thrushes

Herons and Egrets

and more.

I'd love feedback to help make the books informative and enjoyable.

Robin Redbreast

My Little Nature Books, No. 1

2nd Edition

Copyright © 2023 David John Murray

All rights reserved. No part of this publication may be reproduced, stored in a retrieval system, or transmitted in any form by any means, electronic, mechanical, photocopying, recording or otherwise, without the prior permission of the publisher.

All photographs except where specifically noted were taken by myself, the author, and are subject to copyright. Copies of some of them, including framed wall art, can be purchased at Picfair and more will be added from time to time..
https://www.picfair.com/users/DavidMurray/albums

First published: April 2023
2nd Edition: December 2023

ISBN: 9798872565147
Independently published

David Murray Books
Workington, Cumbria, UK
Email: david@mybirds.blog

Hello!

This was the first book in my new series, which originally was going to be called "My Little *Bird* Books". Now they are called, "My Little *Nature* Books" and here's a second edition with a few changes, mostly replacing photographs that in the first edition didn't print as well as I wanted.

We're going to look in this little book at a much loved little bird, our British Robin. Actually, the correct English language name for our Robin is the European Robin (or scientifically, Erithacus rubecula). It is found all over the continent and even further afield. Our robins are quite different from the American Robin, as we'll see on the next page.

I hope you enjoy this little book. After reading it you can test what you've learned by doing the crossword puzzle at the end.

The American Robin (above- photo supplied by a friend in Canada) is a different species from our robins in the British Isles (below). It has a black face and the red of the breast extends further down the body with no white on the front. It is also much larger, close to the size of a blackbird.

How many Robins are there?

Firstly we also have to ask, How many different kinds of robin are there?

On the page opposite is an American Robin, very different in appearance from the European Robin. Occasionally one is blown by strong winds across the Atlantic (known as a "vagrant") but this is very rare.

These are only two of many robins around the world. While the American Robin and also the White-throated Robin of the Middle East are red-breasted, some parts of the world have robins with no red at all; for example the Siberian Blue Robin.

There are many species of robin in Australia that are quite unrelated to the European Robin. Very few of them have anything like the red and white colouring of the European Robin.

But how many are there? A lot! The American Robin population alone is over 350 million, and the European Robin number is probably over 150 million, including around 6 million nesting pairs in Britain (see page 26).

In this little book we'll focus on the European Robin. There are small colour differences between birds from Central Europe, Scandinavia and Britain. They are all the same species but the international ornithology organisations recognise several sub-species. Our British/Irish birds are *Erithacus rubecula melophilus*.

How did the Robin get its name?

Later in the book I tell a story about a robin and "Danny the Dunnock". This is very similar to how our bird, the Robin, got its name. It was a nickname.

In the distant past this little bird with the orange-red face and breast was simply known as a "Redbreast". Other birds with red on them were given similar names, for example Redpoll and Redwing.

Around four hundred years ago the Redbreast started to be given the boy's name Robin. "Robin Redbreast" was at first a nickname, but gradually Robin became accepted as the bird's proper name.

The word "orange" was never used in English until recent centuries. By then the bird name was already "Redbreast" so it was never called an "Orange-breast".

The scientific Latin name was fixed around 1800. Erithacus was an ancient Greek bird name for a robin, while rubecula comes from the Latin word for red.

There are other ancient names. Years ago I met a man with the surname Ruddock. I had no idea then that this was another name for the robin, just as other people have surnames like Falcon, Swan and Wren. The old bird name Ruddock comes from "ruddy", meaning red.

Surprisingly it is only about 50 years since Robin rather than Redbreast became the bird's official English language name.

The Robin's Appearance

A robin is difficult to miss with its red breast and face, and white below, but from behind it is just a dull brown bird that blends in with the branches.

Very often a robin will stand almost upright, with its small body on its quite long legs looking slim and sleek like the one opposite. Sometimes it will have its tail up rather like a wren, as in the photo below.

In cold weather robins can fluff up their feathers to keep warm, looking rather like little red and white balls, as in the lower photo opposite.

Adult males and females look the same. It is almost impossible to look at a robin and tell whether it is male or female. Young ones (juveniles) are different and don't yet have the red face and breast (see page 25.)

Where Do We See Robins?

Here are some of the places that I see robins. The top picture opposite is of a wood where I often spot one, even when I don't see many other birds. In fact several of the pictures in this book were taken close to this path.

The lower image is of a cycle path on an old railway line; people still talk of walking "up the line". There are shrubs and trees along the sides and I have many pictures of robins feeding on the verges and the embankment. In some parts the ground slopes downwards away from the path and the robins often disappear over the bank into the brambles thicket.

The photo below was taken in a garden. This robin perched on the washing line post right next to us while another was on a fence post a short distance away. Maybe they were a pair, or possibly opposite ends of the garden were separate territories.

Robin Behaviour

Robins are often, although not always, confident and friendly with humans. Gardeners, as they dig, often see robins standing by them waiting for a juicy worm to appear. They'll even perch on the spade if it's left alone for a few minutes. With a camera I've been allowed closer to a robin than to any other bird.

Robins, however, are not always gentle birds. They can be violent. An important part of a robin's behaviour is the defence of its territory. Each male robin tries to claim an area as his own.

During the Spring this is because he has a nice female mate and is determined to keep her. He doesn't want to lose his partner to another bird, and his defensive tactics can become quite vicious. Robins with feathers missing are often seen, and two robins may sometimes fight even until one of them is killed.

In Winter he still has to defend his patch. Food is scarce. He doesn't want other birds stealing from his supply of nourishment. Survival through the cold months is hard, and his competitors now are not only other robins but other ground-feeding birds such as Dunnocks (which used to be called Hedge Sparrows).

I like the photo opposite as he looks straight into the camera from a very short distance, coming confidently toward me as I crouch down to set the camera almost at bird's eye level.

Robin's Kingdom - A True Story

Walking near the shore of Windermere in Cumbria recently I spotted Reggie the Robin standing proudly on a green moss-covered rock and flitting from time to time onto a nearby log. Soon he flew away a short distance to forage for grubs under a tree. He'd only been away for a few seconds when Danny the Dunnock decided to occupy the kingdom.

Reggie spotted what was happening and suddenly became a tornado, flying furiously to his rock. Danny didn't wait around. He slunk away quietly.

Soon Reggie went off again. Even the king has to eat, and food was over by the tree among the leaves. The same thing happened again, ... and again, ... and again. As I left Reggie was landing on his log, looking bold, as if to say, "I'm still the king of this castle. No Dunnock is taking my territory!"

What Do Robins Eat?

Robins are often to be seen on the ground in grassy areas and under trees searching for grubs and insects. They love ants, beetles and worms, and will also take other soft (invertebrate) creatures such as spiders, caterpillars, slugs and snails. In a garden there will often be a robin sitting close to where someone is digging, waiting to see what edible creatures appear.

Some kinds of seeds and soft fruits also form part of a robin's diet. Depending on the time of year these may be around half the daily diet. A robin doesn't have a strong seed-crunching bill like some other birds. It will generally look for softer food.

After chicks have hatched from their eggs the mother bird will sometimes break the shells down small and eat them, so "recycling" the calcium back into her body.

In Winter when the ground is frozen hard or covered in snow robins forage for food in shady spots and under leaf litter that has protected the soil underneath from the frost. One may even be found by shallow water taking small fish. This is not their usual way but as the old saying goes, necessity is the mother of invention. Robins are intelligent birds.

Winters are hard for young robins. Much depends on the weather, the availability of food and the bird's ability to find it. Bird tables can help (see page 26).

What do Robins do in Winter?

Many of the Robins that we see in winter months will have started life here during either the previous summer or the one before and stayed at home for the Winter. However a few, maybe one out of every twenty and mostly females, spend winter in France, Spain or Portugal then fly home in the early Spring.

During the winter months we also see migrant robins from Northern Europe, where winters can be extremely cold. This increases our robin population for a few months. Others don't stay here for the whole winter but in Autumn and Spring we see them as they pass through on their migratory journeys.

The Breeding Season

As Spring arrives the top item on a young male robin's mind is to find a mate. The birds here are singing from high branches to attract females, in competition with other males. If they succeed they will stay together as a pair for that year.

A nest is built in some secluded spot, and robins are noted for nesting in the most unusual places. Soon eggs are laid, usually from 4 to 6, one per day. During this time the male hunts for food and helps to feed his mate. The female then incubates the eggs. After two weeks they hatch. Usually robins have two broods per year, sometimes three, and rarely four.

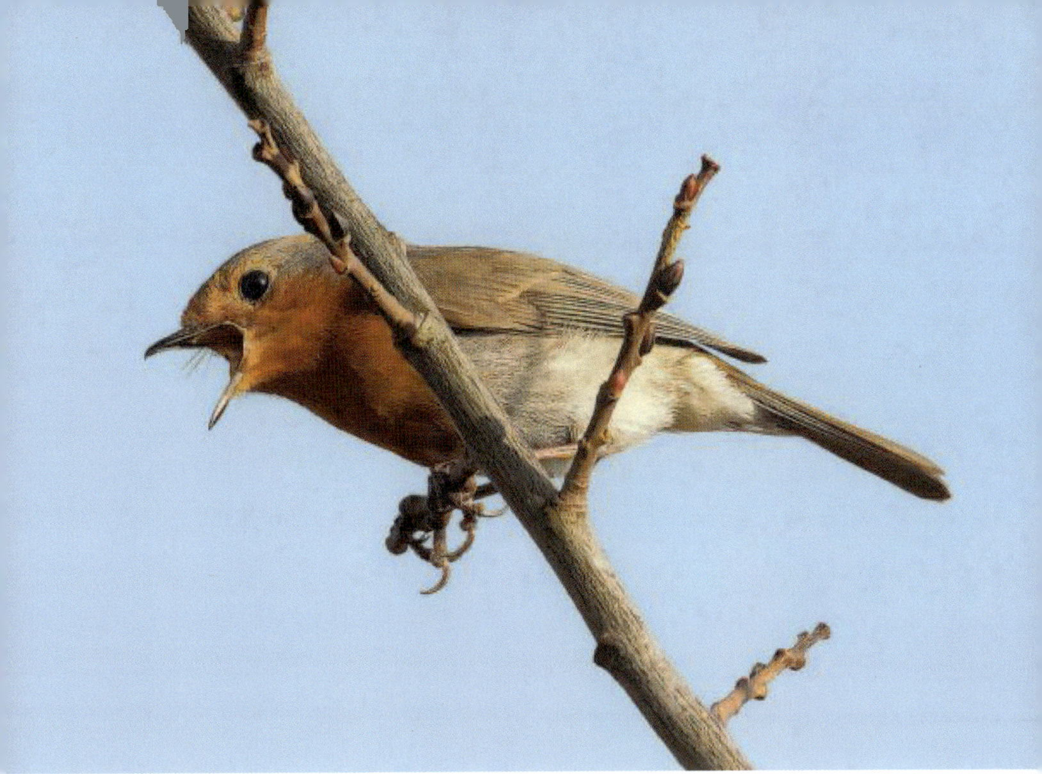
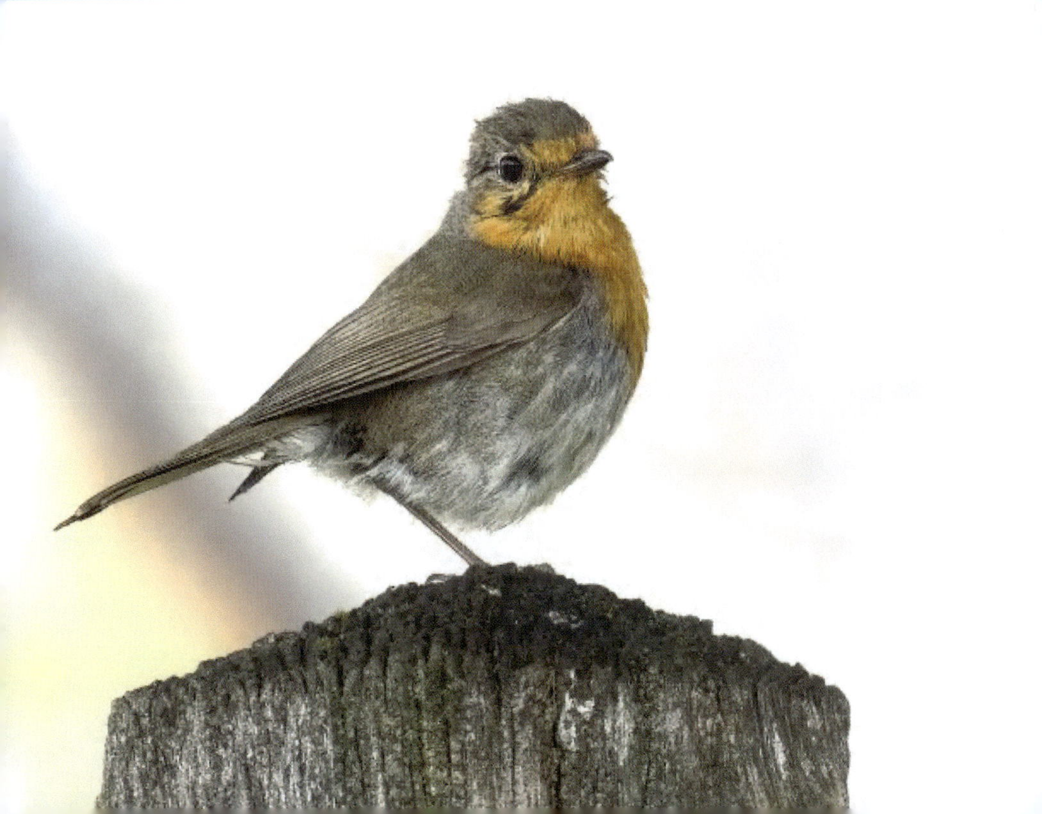

Parents and the Next Generation

When first hatched young robins have no feathers. They are blind and helpless. The parents share the task of caring for them and over the next two weeks they grow their first feathers then soon begin to fly.

By its first winter a young robin has to care for itself, and there is much to learn about surviving the winter months. Severe weather can lead to a big drop in the number of young birds.There are also hungry predators to avoid.

Sadly, most juvenile robins never make it to their first year as a young adult. Few live much more than two or three years. The robin's life is short. Many of the redbreasts we see early in a year, like the one on the left, are the few that survived their first Winter.

This young robin is just starting to show some orange.

Population - Are Robins "At Risk"?

At a time when many bird species are being declared "At Risk" and red-listed it is good to know that the Robin is green-listed. Its population is holding up well, with about 6 million nesting pairs in the UK.

As we saw earlier, only about a quarter of young robins survive their first winter. Freezing weather with little natural food available makes it impossible for a young inexperienced bird to maintain its body weight. Small birds have little fat reserve. This is soon used up if not continually replenished. Garden feeders and bird tables can help if the right foods are put out, they're placed so as to fairly safe from predators, and they're kept clean.

In the wild the predators include small mammals like stoats and weasels as well as birds of prey such as Sparrowhawk and Kestrel. In towns and villages the main culprits are domestic cats. In Britain over a million robins each year are killed by pet cats.

The average life-span of a European Robin is only two or three years although some live longer. So how do robins manage to keep up their numbers?

To put it simply, they have large families. A pair may have several broods of chicks in a year, and with four, five or six chicks in each this compensates for the low survival rate, and at present the population is being maintained very well.

Robins in Poetry

Robin Redbreast has long been a popular symbol of nature in English literature. From William Shakespeare to William Wordsworth and ever since, poets have used this bird as a symbol of hope, renewal, and the beauty of the natural world.

The robin in the Middle Ages became associated with the passion of Christ and was often depicted in religious paintings. Later, during the Victorian era, it became a symbol of Christmas and still today is often seen on Christmas cards and in festive decorations.

The great 19th century poet, William Wordsworth, mentioned robins in some of his poems. Watching butterflies and birds in an orchard one day he wrote, "The Redbreast Chasing The Butterfly", in which he rebukes the robin for pursuing such a beautiful insect. In another, "The Redbreast", he describes how they decided not to have cats in their home, and as the weather became colder in Autumn the robins from the garden would come into the house.

William Cowper, in "A Winter Walk", wrote of the robin's less enthusiastic singing in this colder season:

"The Redbreast warbles still, but is content
With slender notes, and more than half suppressed."

The robin, still often known as Redbreast even today, has been a much loved little bird through many centuries of English literature. Long may it continue.

CROSSWORD

Twenty Questions on Robins

You'll find all the answers in the earlier pages

Enjoy the puzzle

Twenty Robin Questions

Across

2. American cousin's face

4. A robin does this when another bird trespasses on his patch

6. Robins do this in Spring and Summer

8. A dangerous time for young robins

11. Changing feathers

14. First word (the genus) of the robin's scientific name

15. We like to hear this from a robin

16. This keeps robins very busy early in the year

18. Trained experts may put a very lightweight one on a robin's leg

19. One place where a robin might have its home

20. A country where some British robins spend winter months

Down

1. The chick is learning to fly

3. Popular name for the robin

5. A favourite food in the robin family

7. An ancient name for the robin

9. Used in ringing birds but only by trained and licensed people

10. Just a small minority of British robins do this in autumn

12. When other food is scarce robins have been known to eat small ones

13. A main item in the robin's diet

17. The conservation status of the robin in Britain.

Bird Photography

Before we finish I should say a little about bird photography. Firstly, there is no need to have the latest expensive camera and lenses. A new modern camera might make it possible to take photos in difficult conditions, such as poor light or from a far distance, but much is possible with older equipment.

I always suggest that people should start with a fairly inexpensive camera and see what they can do with it. If you have money available you could try to get a secondhand older SLR (single lens reflex) camera such as a Nikon D3200 or 3500 with a 300mm zoom lens from a camera shop or online.

I originally used a fifteen year old Nikon D3000 with which I'd previously done landscape photography. Many of the bird images were good enough for printing and looked very respectable on social media. If your budget doesn't stretch to that you could look for a secondhand "bridge" camera with a built-in zoom Try it and see. It's great fun. It takes practice, but keep at it and you'll get better, even on dull days.

The image opposite is a little hazy but is actually quite realistic. It was taken on a dismal drizzly day at a nature reserve. As another example see the one below, of a Tree Creeper climbing up a wall to visit Robin. This had to be taken with no warning and no delay, and it's one of my favourite photos from 2022.

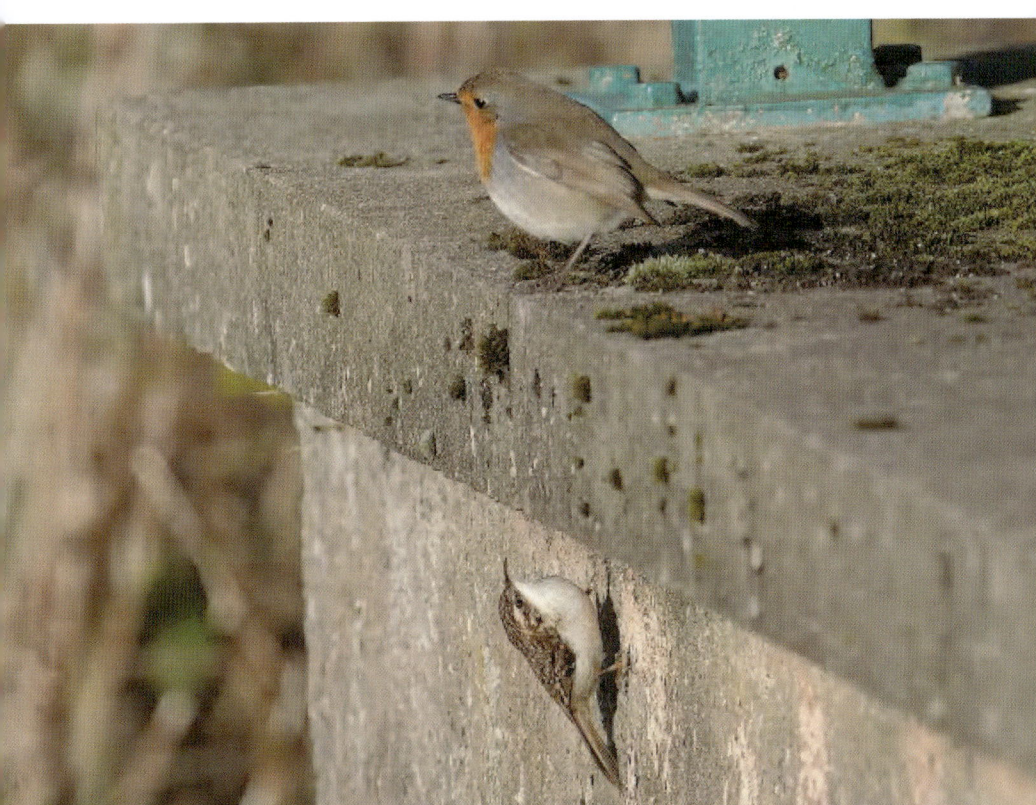

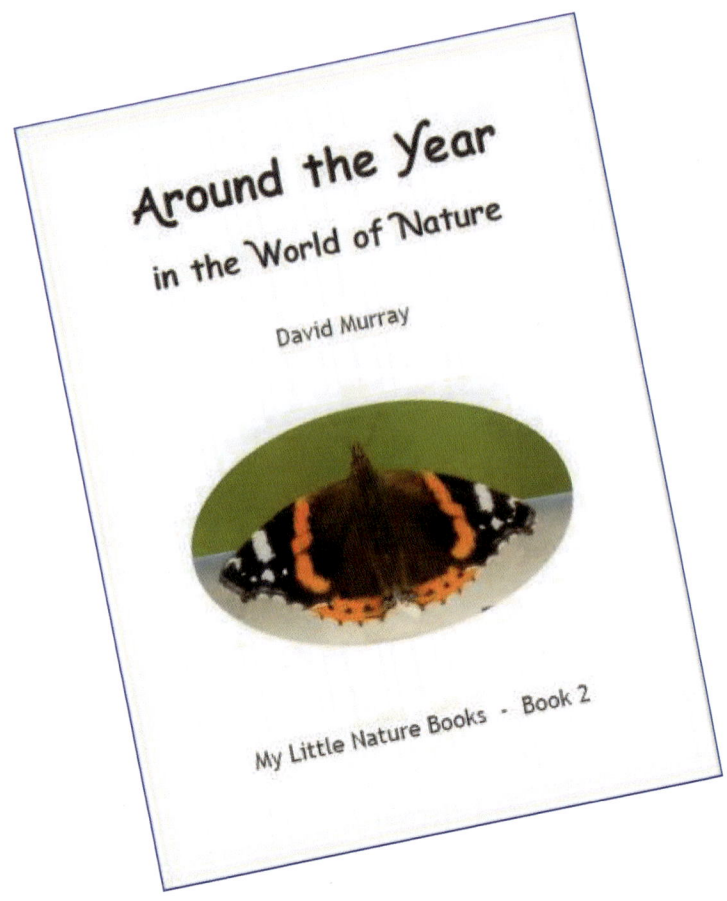

The second book in the series

Around the Year in the World of Nature

is now available from Amazon in paperback

and early in 2024 as a Kindle ebook.

More are being being planned

Goldfinch and Other Finches

Blackbird and other Thrushes

Curlew and other Waders

"Some Of My Birds"
Avian Therapy Close to Home

After publishing some of my bird photographs on social media for a couple of years several friends suggested that I should put them into a book. For Christmas 2022 I assembled a hundred pages into a paperback edition and shared this with friends and family.

Packed with photographs of birds of coast, pond, river and woodland near home in West Cumbria it also includes some of my experiences in learning more both about the birds themselves and the techniques of photographing them. The response has been so good that I'm now taking it further.

Feedback on the 1st (Limited) Edition:

- "Thank you for the lovely book. I've been enjoying reading it." (D.C., Lancashire)
- "I couldn't put it down. Were all these different birds really within a few miles of home? I've read it through twice." (A near neighbour).
- "What a lovely book, so well presented, and such lovely photographs." (M.H., Carlisle)

So watch out for the 2nd edition (actually the first to be given any publicity) coming in mid-2024, now to be 180-200 pages and including photographs of birds seen in places further afield, firstly in hardback then later in both paperback and Kindle ebook formats.

Printed in Great Britain
by Amazon